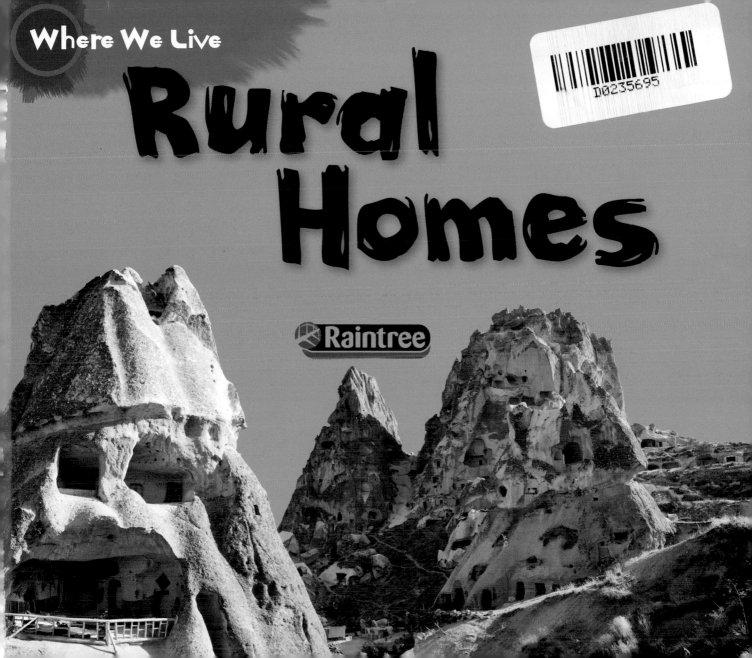

Rural Homes

Raintree

Raintree is an imprint of Capstone Global Library Limited, a company incorporated in England and Wales having its registered office at 7 Pilgrim Street, London, EC4V 6LB – Registered company number: 6695582

To contact Raintree:
Phone: 0845 6044371
Fax: + 44 (0) 1865 312263
Email: myorders@raintreepublishers.co.uk
Outside the UK please telephone +44 1865 312262.

Edited by Daniel Nunn and Abby Colich
Designed by Cynthia Akiyoshi
Picture research by Mica Brancic
Production by Sophia Argyris
Originated by Capstone Global Library
Printed and bound in China at RR Donnelly Asia Printing Solutions

ISBN 978-1-4062-6322-0
17 16 15 14 13
10 9 8 7 6 5 4 3 2 1

British Library Cataloguing in Publication Data
Smith, Sian.
  Rural homes. -- (Where we live)
  1. Country homes--Juvenile literature.
  I. Title II. Series
  643.1'091734-dc23

Acknowledgements
We would like to thank the following for permission to reproduce photographs: Getty Images pp. 4 (National Geographic/Joy Tessman); 6, 23 bottom (Flickr/Ulrike Maier); 7, 23 centre bottom (AWL Images/Peter Adams); 9 (Robert Harding World Imagery/Eurasia); 12, 23 top (AFP Photo/Sabah Arar); 14 (AFP Photo/Rizwan Tabassum); 15 (Lonely Planet Images/Aldo Pavan); 16, 22 bottom right (Oxford Scientific/Trevor Worden); 18, 22 bottom left (Robert Harding World Imagery/Dallas & John Heaton); 19 (Photographer's Choice RF/Cristian Baitg); 20, 22 top right (Digital Vision/John Clutterbuck); 21, 23 centre top (Lonely Planet Images/Mark Daffey); Shutterstock pp. 5 (© Rob Marmion); 8 (© Radu Razvan); 10 (© S Reynolds); 11 (© Chrislofoto); 13, 22 top left (© iPics); SuperStock p. 17 (hemi/Hemis.fr/Franck Guiziou).

Front cover photograph of huts of the Tairona Indians, Colombia, reproduced with permission of Shutterstock (© urosr). Back cover photograph of a log cabin in Lapland, Finland reproduced with permission of Shutterstock (© iPics).

Every effort has been made to contact copyright holders of material reproduced in this book. Any omissions will be rectified in subsequent printings if notice is given to the publisher.

Contents

Why do people need homes?

People live in homes.

Homes keep people safe.

What does rural mean?

village

When something is rural, it is in the countryside. Villages are in rural places.

Rural places are far away from cities and large towns.

Rural homes

There is more space to keep animals and grow plants in rural places.

farmhouse

Some people live on farms.

Some people live on ranches.

Some rural homes are large and have big gardens.

What are rural homes made of?

reeds

People sometimes use the materials around them to build rural homes.

log cabin

Many homes are made of wood.

Some homes are made of mud
or clay.

stone

Some homes are made of stone or brick.

Unusual rural homes

stilts

Some homes are on stilts.

Some homes float on water.

Some homes are under the ground.

Some homes are in caves.

Neighbours

Some people in rural homes live far away from their neighbours.

Some people in rural homes live close to their neighbours.

Around the world

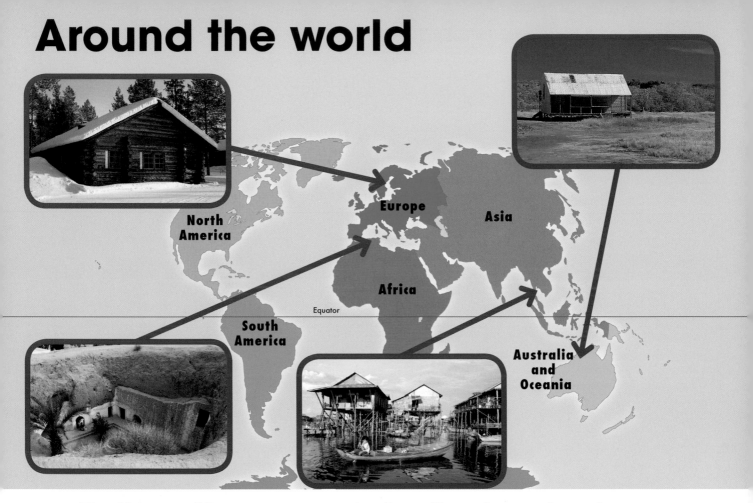

North America

Europe

Asia

Africa

Equator

South America

Australia and Oceania

Follow the arrows to find out where each of these homes are.

More information on page 24

Picture glossary

material what something is made from. Wood and stone are types of material.

neighbours people who live near to you

rural countryside or places far away from cities

village place where people live in the counryside. A village is smaller than a town.

Index

Photograph information

The photographs in this book were taken from the following locations: p. 4 Namibia, Africa; p. 5 Viñales, Cuba; p. 6 Longsheng province, China; p. 7 Ethiopia, Africa; p. 8 the Alps, Switzerland; p. 9 Gwynedd, Wales; p. 11 England; p. 12 Najaf, Iraq; p. 13 Lapland, Finland; p. 14 Hyderabad, Pakistan; p. 15 Dang village, China; p. 16 floating village on Tonle Sap, Cambodia; p. 17 Chong Khneas floating village, Cambodia; p. 18 Matmata, Tunisia; p. 19 Uchisar Capadoccia, Turkey; p. 20 Broome, Australia; p. 21 Amantani Island, Peru.

Notes for parents and teachers

Introduce the children to the word *rural*. Explain that rural places are in the countryside where there's lots of space and fewer buildings (unlike cities and towns) and that there are rural places all over the world. Read the book together and ask the children what they think it might be like to live in the different types of rural home. Discuss the materials the homes are made from and any special features. For example, homes made from mud or clay and homes that are under the ground tend to stay cool in hot weather. Look at the pictures on pages 20 and 21 together. Why do the children think it would be important to have good neighbours when you live in a rural place? Encourage the children to draw a picture of their favourite type of rural home and to write a sentence describing it.